Cross-System Collaboration: Tools That Work

by James L. Hoel

CWLA Press • Washington, DC

CWLA Press is an imprint of the Child Welfare League of America. The Child Welfare League of America (CWLA) is a privately supported, non-profit, membership-based organization committed to preserving, protecting, and promoting the well-being of all children and their families. Believing that children are our most valuable resource, CWLA, through its membership, advocates for high standards, sound public policies, and quality services for children in need and their families.

CHILD WELFARE LEAGUE OF AMERICA, INC.
440 First Street, NW, Third Floor, Washington, DC 20001-2085
E-mail: books@cwla.org

CURRENT PRINTING (last digit)
10 9 8 7 6 5 4 3 2 1

Cover design by Jenny Geanakos

Printed in the United States of America

ISBN # 0–87868-715-7

Contents

Acknowledgments

This manuscript is the result of a collaborative process. Far from representing the thoughts of one author, the ideas discussed here are based on many hours of interviews with community leaders working in cross-system collaborative initiatives in Iowa. For their hard work, and for taking the additional time to reflect back on their work together, I need to extend formal recognition to the following individuals:

- **District administration:** Marlie Kasemeier, Iowa Department of Human Services; Steve Smith, First Judicial District Juvenile Court Services; James Ernst, Four Oaks of Iowa.

- **Waterloo, Iowa:** Jan Pratt, Waterloo Region Department of Human Services; Sue Pitts-Fisher, Four Oaks; Evan Klenk, Waterloo Area Department of Human Services; Kevin Wahl, Blackhawk County Juvenile Court Services; Anne Gruenewald, Four Oaks; Denise Dunn, Waterloo Area Decategorization Project.

- **Oelwein, Iowa:** Steve Buschbaum, Fayette County Juvenile Court Services; Art Finnigan, Fayette County Department of Human Services; Pam Brown, Fayette County Department of Human Services; Tim Gilson, Oelwein Community School District; Janet Freeman, Tricounty Decategorization Project.

- **Dubuque, Iowa:** Tom Hoelscher, Dubuque County Juvenile Court Services; Dane Schrobilgen, Four Oaks; Mike Mitchell, Four Oaks; Gary Lippe, Dubuque County Department of Human Services; Dave Olson, Dubuque Community School District; Sue Davison, Dubuque County Decategorization Project.

- **Project consultants:** Dennis Braziel, Child Welfare League of America, and Bill Roach, Iowa Attorney General's Task Force on Juvenile Crime.

Introduction

Over the past several years, the Child Welfare League of America (CWLA) has sought to expand the degree to which parents of children in out-of-home care are involved in programs and in decision-making. One result has been the CWLA Out-of-Home Care Task Force, a group that identified many of the significant issues that are raised by increased family involvement in traditionally child-centered service systems.

In 1992, CWLA convened a Family Focus Forum to respond to the Task Force report and consider the issues involved in helping traditional, child-centered social service agencies move to a stronger family-based orientation. This Forum laid the groundwork for addressing such topics as impacts on agency culture, staff role changes, needs for training and re-training, program integration priorities, and funding dilemmas.

CWLA's next initiative, "Mapping a New Direction: Bringing Families into Traditional Child Welfare Services," built on the work accomplished in the Family Focus Forum. "Mapping I" developed programs of comprehensive training, technical assistance, and consulting services designed to assist child welfare agencies adopt family-focused practices that would enhance the child welfare services they provide. One important product of this initiative was the publication, *Family-Focused Practice in Out-of-Home Care: A Handbook and Resources Directory* [Braziel 1996]. Four Oaks, a private nonprofit comprehensive family service agency here in Iowa, contributed a chapter to this handbook describing its efforts to provide a model family-focused residential treatment program for preadolescents [Gruenewald 1996].

In 1996, CWLA established a follow-up initiative, "Mapping a New Direction II: Forging Collaborative Partnerships to Support Family-Focused Out-of-Home Care." "Mapping II" assisted voluntary agencies to develop tools and strategies to strengthen collaborative relationships among public and private child welfare agencies (as well as other stakeholders) as they move toward a family-focused philosophy.

As participants in "Mapping a New Direction II," Four Oaks and the Iowa Department of Human Services formed a public-private partnership to design a demonstration project illustrating not only a family-based "wrap-around" service program that would divert identified youth from residential care, but also a fully collaborative program model that exemplified a neighborhood focus for designing and providing comprehensive services to families. The tools used and lessons learned during this first Iowa case study have been documented in a monograph, authored by Anne Gruenewald and published by CWLA [Gruenewald 1998].

In 1997, CWLA once again extended their work in this important field by cosponsoring, in collaboration with the Annie E. Casey Foundation, a third initiative, "Mapping a New Direction III: Strategies to Enhance Family-Centered Public/Private Partnerships." This initiative had the following goals:

- To develop a series of "how-to" practical strategies for successful collaboration;

- To prepare a series of monographs that illustrate emerging public-private partnerships;

- To provide onsite consultation, technical assistance, and program evaluations; and

- To assist state, county, and local leaders to plan and convene forums for key community constituents involved in service delivery for at-risk children and families.

Once again, here in Iowa, the Iowa Department of Human Services and Four Oaks, working with the state's First Judicial District Juvenile Court Services Administration, committed to continue their involvement with "Mapping a New Direction." Believing that the previous demonstration project in Waterloo was successful, the chief administrators from all three agencies decided to continue their collaboration with specific emphasis on services to delinquent and at-risk adolescents. These agencies also agreed to extend this initiative across 11 northern counties that comprise the overlap of the First Judicial District and the Waterloo Regional Office of the Iowa Department of Human Services.

The Project

Iowa's "Mapping a New Direction III" project involved two key components. The first component, **a series of community forums**, sought to widen the scope of participation in community planning to meet the needs of at-risk youth in three Iowa communities: Waterloo, Oelwein, and Dubuque. All three communities are at different stages in developing Decategorization Projects—the statewide movement toward devolution that establishes increased collaborative local control for the planning and fiscal management of each community-level human service delivery system (see Chapter 1 for more information on decategorization). Furthermore, all three communities have experienced success in recent years with innovative treatment and preventative service designs, specifically in the field of juvenile justice. All three communities have been involved in high levels of collaborative work.

The primary purpose for the forums has been to increase community awareness and participation. Each one-day forum involved more than 100 local representatives in critically examining the continuum of services available to delinquent youth and their families in each community. The forums also provided opportunities for these representatives to reach consensus on which aspects of the local service continuum needed to receive time, attention, resources, and strengthening. Resource people from a number of state and national organizations collaborated to participate in each event:

- The Iowa Attorney General's Task Force on Juvenile Crime;
- The Iowa Human Rights Commission;
- The Office of Juvenile Justice and Delinquency Prevention, Office of Justice Programs, U.S. Department of Justice; and
- The Child Welfare League of America.

Each community placed primary emphasis on actively recruiting representatives from key stakeholders who are not traditionally included in human services planning and needs assessment activities:

- Business leaders,

- The local religious community,
- Senior citizens,
- Client families,
- Foster families,
- Officers of the court,
- Law enforcement professionals,
- Neighborhood organizations, and
- Other indigenous citizens' groups concerned with juvenile justice and child welfare issues.

The second key component of Iowa's "Mapping a New Direction III" project seeks **to develop a "toolbox"** of effective principles for collaboration that can be of practical assistance to families, agencies, and communities, as each addresses the challenges of system reform. Over the past several years, each of the three Iowa communities participating in this project (Waterloo, Oelwein, and Dubuque) have experienced considerable success in creating effective cross-system collaboratives to manage important new community-based juvenile justice programs and, in the case of the Decategorization Projects, to begin to manage the total local service delivery system through a more collaborative design.

As part of the "Mapping a New Direction III" project, community leaders were asked to participate in a series of structured interviews and to reflect on the successes they have achieved together in what they themselves identify as their most effective collaborative activities. This study attempts to summarize, in concise form, the insights developed through this interview process.

Purpose

The purpose of this monograph, then, is to provide a set of brief discussions of "tools that work"—practice principles that can be useful to those who engage in the challenge of integrating human services through various designs of cross-system collaboration.

The underlying framework for the discussion is pragmatic and empirical—as collaborative work itself should be. No theoretical preconceptions were allowed to guide what were, essentially, open-ended interviews.

Having said this, I must give credit to Sharon Kagan's seminal work on systems integration [Kagan 1993]. Due to Kagan's own empirical and practical orientation, as well as her substantive contributions to this new field of study, some baseline influence becomes almost unavoidable.

Beyond this, I confess to a clinical background in residential group work and family counseling. So while conducting interviews, I found it difficult *not* to be reminded of the basic premise of general systems theory. A system is a system is a system. A group is a group is a group. There are general properties that govern how systems behave and these principles can be generalized from one system to another. For example, just as "boundary issues" are critical to understanding children, families, and adolescent peer groups in residential treatment, so are "boundary issues" critical to understanding both communities and the dynamics of collaborative work groups. For example, the notion of "parallel process" is a powerful tool in understanding how one system relates to another, whether this is a clinical understanding of a family or a political understanding of a state system.

Hopefully, this kind of awareness can encourage other treatment practitioners as they set sail on what often feels like the uncharted waters of community-based collaborative activities.

In addition, as I sorted through the interview data, I found a strong tendency to prioritize the obvious. Often, comments in interviews were accompanied by such disclaimers as, "This point must be obvious," or "This impression is only common sense." My bias is to include the ideas to which such disclaimers were attached. The purpose here is not to be clever or unique. Our outcomes affect real children, real families, and real pain. To the extent that a tool for effective collaboration begins to feel so obvious that it is hardly worth discussion, it is probably powerful. As William Glasser, a patron saint of residential treatment, once observed, "Reality therapy is not difficult to understand; it is, however, very difficult to do" [Glasser 1967].

Finally, it should be emphasized that the discussion that follows embraces a strengths-based philosophy. Consideration was, in fact, given to a format that would include "barriers" and strategies to overcome them. Instead, for purposes of modeling, our emphasis is placed squarely on "what works."

The Iowa Context

As Sharon Kagan points out, cross-system integration initiatives must be conceptualized as a complex pattern of reciprocal state-local interactions. Each state's demographic, historical, economic, political, and ideological context will fundamentally shape the course and direction of local system reform activities [Kagan et al. 1995].

Unfortunately, the very nature of systems reform in the direction of cross-system integration, with its attendant emphasis on smaller, manageable collaboratives and close, personal partnerships, tends to emphasize local, neighborhood, or even interpersonal dynamics at the expense of larger-system issues, leadership, and policies. Indeed, larger systems too often are viewed as the very evil that reform efforts seek to deconstruct: bureaucratic, dysfunctional, impersonal, and intrinsically frustrating to customers, consumers, and providers of services alike. This implicit demonization of larger systems leads Hagebak and others to conclude that service integration efforts must focus exclusively on a local level and, in the context of this study, leads most interview respondents to discuss local and interpersonal dynamics as the critical focus for "tools that work" [Hagebak 1979].

Prior to examining local issues and practical hands-on collaboration strategies, much can be learned from a brief overview of the larger Iowa context.

Field-Driven Restructuring

Iowa has experienced long-term, consistent political leadership in human services. Republican Governor Terry Brandstad is now completing his fourth term of office, and Director of Human Services Charles M. Palmer has held his position for more than 12 years, longer than any Human Services Commissioner in the state's history. Palmer, early on, announced that his long-term administrative strategy would be field driven. That is, his intent was to reduce the Department of Human Services (DHS) centralized administration and to delegate increased responsibility and control to local jurisdictions. This philosophy was implemented, over time, through a series of DHS restructurings, each of which reduced the number of DHS regional offices, reduced DHS middle-management staff positions, and shifted DHS administrative control to regional and county human service administrators. While not overtly dictating a collaborative service model, Palmer's field-driven approach clearly has supported integrative innovations by placing considerable decisionmaking latitude at a local level and by reducing levels of bureaucracy in the overall service system.

Fiscal Accountability

Iowa, like other states, has historically struggled to gain fiscal control of its human services expenditures, specifically in the area of entitlements. From a child welfare perspective, problems relating to fiscal control were exacerbated when the state enacted juvenile justice and child welfare legislation in 1978. This legislation, which placed the ability to control child placement in the hands of the Juvenile Court, was passed in response to the federal Crime and Delinquency Act of 1974. Iowa later reinforced the Court's centrality when the legislature responded to federal permanency planning mandates by expanding the Court's ability to determine level of care, order specific treatment modalities, and monitor cases within its jurisdiction at six-month intervals. Assigning case control to the courts and fiscal responsibility to DHS created a division that dominated the political landscape of Iowa's human service arena for more than 15 years. Not coincidentally, this same time period saw an exponential increase in child welfare services, including family-centered services, residential treatment, and treatment foster care. Given the understanding that group care and foster care were entitlements, and with juvenile courts ordering children into placement on the basis of the best interest of the child, Iowa's child welfare budget was effectively out of control.

In 1993, Governor Brandstad and Commissioner Palmer developed a legal base to assert that group foster care was *not* an entitlement and successfully crafted legislation to cap group care expenditures and, by implication, the state's total child welfare budget. While this position is currently weakened to some degree by recent Iowa Supreme Court rulings, group care capitation has had dramatic impact on the Iowa child welfare system over the past five years.

First, this legislation strongly reinforced the field-driven administrative structure outlined above. DHS county directors now held both the responsibility to control county budgets and increased authority to carry out this responsibility. Second, under the specific provisions of the legislation that capped group care expenditures, dollars could be transferred from the group care line item to preventative and family-centered services, but could not be transferred from other line items into the group care budget. Together, these two factors strengthened community autonomy and challenged communities to develop creative local alternatives to out-of-home care.

Decategorization

Iowa's efforts to decategorize funding streams (DECAT) have been cautious, but now, 10 years into the process, these efforts have become well-entrenched and will likely dominate the future of Iowa's human services delivery system.

Iowa DECAT began with five pilot projects that encouraged—but did not mandate—local jurisdictions to blend service dollars. Each county received a small budget earmarked for decategorization programs. This budget could be voluntarily augmented from DHS categorical line items, Juvenile Court categorical line items, public school "at-risk" line items, substance abuse agency dollars, and (at least conceptually) funding from any other community agency or program, such as public health or mental health services. Decategorized dollars could be used flexibly and with discretion by a local Board of Governance that represented DHS, the Juvenile Court, and the County Board of Supervisors. Perhaps most significantly, local communities were offered an incentive to succeed: unlike categorical dollars that revert to the state's general fund when unspent, decategorized dollars could "carry over" to the next fiscal year.

The state DECAT strategy is clearly flawed by its design as a program of attraction, rather than compulsion. While Juvenile Court and DHS have, in many jurisdictions, found common ground in the DECAT projects, few other agencies have voluntarily chosen to blend dollars. However, DECAT has been instrumental in reconceptualizing field-driven local control as an essentially collaborative process that provides multiple agency stakeholders with incentives to work together to assess service needs and develop innovative program initiatives. Today, more than 90% of Iowa counties are involved in the DECAT strategy, and current legislative planning indicates that this devolutionary and collaborative design will be strengthened in future years [Funero et al. 1998].

Public Partners: Juvenile Court/DHS Integration

Historically, Iowa's child welfare service system has been defined by the separation of Juvenile Court Services (JCS) to delinquent youth and the child welfare services provided by DHS.

On a case level, significant overlaps have always existed. DHS caseworkers and juvenile probation officers have frequently worked with the same family, but with different children as the identified client. Also, both agencies frequently have worked with the same child and family sequentially. For example, a family may enter the system as a DHS case by virtue of needing services in response to child abuse, and then become a JCS case if the child were later adjudicated delinquent. Interestingly, the same case would revert back to DHS during and following placement in a state training school since, under Iowa Code, the state DHS director assumes legal guardianship through this process.

Closer integration of these two public child-service agencies has been a slow and indirect process. In recent years, Juvenile Court officers and judges have become state employees, rather than employees funded through local jurisdictions. While this has not functionally eroded the authority of the supervisory judge in each judicial district, the change nonetheless has meaning. At a statewide level, DHS regional administrators and chief Juvenile Court officers from each Iowa judicial district have only recently begun to meet on a regularly scheduled basis to review policy issues and to address matters of common concern.

In 1995, the Iowa Legislature created a package of important delinquency-specific services—community treatment, tracking and monitoring, life skills development, and school-based services—and placed the dollars to fund these services under the administration of chief juvenile court officers. This initiative empowered juvenile court management staff and gave them more in common with their DHS peers. Not only were both agencies case managers and service providers, but both agencies were now public service administrators, and both were dealing with significant budget responsibilities, prerogatives, and opportunities.

As Tom Hoelscher, the Dubuque JCS Administrator asserts: "It is the creation of this new funding stream that has most powerfully given impetus to collaboration. As long as each public agency related to different cases, there seemed little need to connect. But when both local managers, DHS and JCS, had meaningful budgets to administer, we had every reason to work together to best use our resources."

Private Partners: The Iowa Coalition

In the private human services sector, Iowa has a long and relatively successful history of state-level private agency cooperation through the Iowa Coalition of Family and Children's Services. This Coalition is more than a lobbying group joined by fiscal self-interest. It has allowed private child welfare agencies, as a collective, to develop an effective social policy presence at the state level.

In terms of private-private partnership, the work of the Iowa Coalition has evolved to include a peer review process and a statewide outcome measurement system. This high degree of state-level collaboration has provided a positive context for local agencies seeking collaborative private-private partnerships to create local initiatives.

At the level of local, cross-systems collaborations, the Coalition creates a similar parallel process dynamic in terms of public-private collaboration. When private agency managers gain credibility in state-level public policy forums, the stage is set for meaningful public-private partnerships at the local level.

Managed Care

Public and private child welfare agencies across the country are becoming reconciled to the presence of managed care in their futures. In Iowa, managed care is a reality today. For many years, psychiatric residential treatment programs have been directly funded through the Medicaid Clinical Option, and the Iowa Foundation for Medical Care (IFMC) performs gatekeeping and concurrent review functions based on the managed care model traditionally used for medical services.

Three years ago, Iowa became the first state to administer a major portion of its human services dollars through a capitated contract with a multinational managed care organization. Today, the Merit Behavioral Care Corporation manages all of Iowa's Public Mental Health Services dollars for children and adults. Legislative debates, even as this account is written, center on the possibility of extending the "Iowa Plan" contract to include all child welfare and juvenile justice services [Oss & Taylor 1997].

These changes have important, multiple impacts on public and private agencies serving Iowa's children.

For **private agencies**, the advent of managed care has created a more competitive environment. Believing that geographic spread and large service capacity may be crucial to future subcontracts with statewide managed care organizations, local private agencies have frequently become regional agencies that offer a full continuum of service to children and families. Local agencies in what had historically been single-agency communities, therefore, have begun to encounter new competition from nonprofit child welfare agencies that have increasingly embraced a businesslike orientation to their service mission. To survive in this competitive environment and continue to help children and families, agencies have become more cost effective and more customer focused.

Interestingly, **public agencies in Iowa** (DHS and JCS) have experienced a similar shift toward a competitive environment. This is most clearly illustrated by recent public policy debates on whether to turn children's services over to a statewide multinational managed care provider or to create an administrative services only (ASO) contract that allows local jurisdictions to enhance "devolved" local control through the purchase of sophisticated management information systems and managed care technology. On the one hand, managed care clearly presents itself as a threat to the autonomy of local jurisdictions. On the other hand, managed care also presents itself as a key resource if, and only if, local jurisdictions can market themselves as credible managers of integrated local service systems, as well as managers of services and dollars.

Managed care, its ethical implications, and its impact on children's services are topics beyond the scope of this study. For our purposes, we look upon managed care as a force that is pushing us toward collaboration and systems integration. In this new, fundamentally competitive environment, private agencies are impelled toward a customer-oriented process of working with their public agency partners to design and provide services that better meet customer and consumer needs. Similarly, public agencies find themselves in competition at the local level with sophisticated state and even multinational managed care organizations. To succeed, they must prove their ability to become good systems managers. These dynamics push public agencies toward greater inclusion of their private agency partners. At the same time, private agencies, no longer the only provider to a local community, must learn to collaborate effectively with their peer agency competitors.

Exemplary Collaborations

As Kagan points out, important impacts on local collaborative initiatives are not limited to state-level, top-down systems issues. Local jurisdictions clearly influence one another through a horizontal (rather than vertical) relationship of reciprocal communication [Kagan et al. 1995]. The clearest example of this kind of influence occurs when one community or one sector of the human service system takes the lead and becomes known as a successful cross-systems collaborative effort.

In Iowa, the FaDDs program, an important initiative in state welfare reform, established neighborhood-based family development centers that provide "one-stop shopping" for low-income families by co-locating critical agencies in the same building: DHS income maintenance workers, federal agency antipoverty workers, federal employment training programs, and grant-funded family support and family development workers, who are charged with the responsibility of integrating family services and developing indigenous support systems for families in the community. FaDDs' programs have "pushed the envelope" of cross-system collaboration in Iowa. Not only have they succeeded in broadening cross-system involvements by developing strong partnerships with schools and corporate sponsors, FaDDs' family development centers have also produced statistically credible outcomes in helping families get out of poverty *and* in preventing child abuse and out-of-home placements for younger children [Bruner 1996].

Iowa's pilot program for delinquency-specific day treatment in Sioux City developed a highly collaborative design that involved blended funding from DHS and JCS, as well as high levels of program integration with the public school. This initiative also piloted the concept of weekly team decisionmaking among private agencies, JCS, and DHS regarding intake and

whether each child should experience day treatment or residential-level structure the next week. In this way, through the Sioux
City experience, delinquency-specific day treatment, early on,
became linked with the value of cross-systems collaboration.

The Oelwein School District received fund-
ing from the state Department of Education to develop the "Huskie
Hub," a freestanding school-based family support program that
co-located private social service agencies, DHS services,
substance abuse services, and remedial education services. The
success of this initiative was in large part related to a highly collaborative community board that represented virtually every stakeholder group in this small community. The "Huskie Hub"
program, in turn, established a positive example and precedent
for the later collaborative Oelwein initiatives to be discussed in
this report.

These and other exemplary collaborative initiatives have shaped
the content and direction of systems reform at a local level here in
Iowa, as one community has influenced another through peer communication and modeling that multiplies exponentially beyond whatever
linear, top-down influence occurs from a state policy level.

Moreover, when many of these exemplary projects emerge simulta-
neously (as has been the case in Iowa), a new practice standard crys-
tallizes. The imperative for collaboration is simply "in the air."

Summary

Successful collaborative efforts are deeply embedded in local communities. As our interview respondents emphasize, again and again, it
is the hard work, the willingness to change, and the willingness to
trust and forge hard-won relationships—actions by particular people
in particular places—that spark each successful collaborative. Respect
for these realities, however, should not prevent us from understanding
how, here in Iowa (as elsewhere), state-level structures, policies, and

programs work to support or to thwart local initiatives. It is in this larger context that we need to examine more specific strategies—the tools that work.

Tools That Work: Structural Elements

As previously observed, general systems theory applies to communities and collaborative boards, as well as to families, individuals, and adolescent peer groups. Not surprisingly, therefore, respondents to each interview situation all identified a number of key structural elements— issues relating to roles, rules, boundaries, and subsystems—that help collaborative partnerships to function as healthy, effective, interpersonal groups.

Blending Funding Streams

As practical managers recognize, money is the lifeblood of any human service organizations, and as Sharon Kalemkiarian, an Anne E. Casey Foundation Consultant and Director of Project Heartbeat in San Diego, teaches us, blending funding streams becomes a powerful force in supporting collaborative work [Kalemkiarian 1996]. When resources are pooled and mutually administered, the fundamental structure of the collaborative relationship is redefined. This is not a cynical view or an adherence to the belief that only money "makes the world go round." It is a correct understanding that effective allocation of fiscal resources is a critical management function. In the field of human services, custodianship of increasingly scarce financial resources becomes, in fact, an ethical imperative. As a result, blending funding streams creates a paradigm shift from competition and conflict to protect "my" dollars, to a structural framework where collaboration is mandated to effectively use "our" dollars. This is a radical redefinition of role, purpose, and relationship. The power of this strategy can not be underestimated.

In some Iowa jurisdictions, delinquency-specific day treatment programs are solely funded and adminis-

17

tered through Juvenile Court Services (JCS). In other jurisdictions, JCS funds some cases, while the Department of Human Services (DHS) funds others. Such configurations foster conflict. If programs are successful in diverting youth from higher cost placements when funds are not blended, the initiative frees DHS dollars that may or may not benefit JCS clients. And when funds are not blended, inclusion of family therapy and brief residential placements for purposes of stabilization and behavior control requires access to DHS dollars to support a JCS program.

By contrast, in the PHASE program design, DHS Regional Administrator Marlie Kasemeier and Chief Juvenile Court Administrator Steve Smith forged an administrative agreement early on, so that each PHASE day treatment case would be jointly supported by DHS and JCS funding streams. These programs were charged to serve not only adjudicated delinquents, but also conduct-disordered adolescents on DHS caseloads. This single administrative agreement helped to bring subordinate supervisors from both agencies to the table and created high levels of ownership for both the day treatment project itself and for the challenge of developing new designs for comanagement.

Equity of Investment

Dollars are not the only resource. In many collaborative projects, blending funding streams is simply not an option. Nonetheless, successful partnerships are rooted in some level of equity of investment, and, therefore, some balance in terms of motivation and influence. Many years ago, family therapists identified the dynamic of marital "skew." Put simply, when one partner in a marriage is more intelligent, more attractive, or more powerful by far, a balanced and functional partnership is an unlikely result [Coleman 1973].

As our interview respondents point out, too often organizational skew is exactly what does happen in many dysfunctional collaborative initiatives. One organization dominates. Other organizations are clearly subordinate, underinvested, or are simply attending another meeting in a busy schedule. At worst, the result can be a hypocritical premise and an empty exercise—the pretense and form of collaboration without its substance.

Innovative programs are developed in many local Iowa jurisdictions by public or private social service agencies and too often educational professionals come to the table as reluctant or second-class participants. By contrast, when funding for delinquency-specific day treatment in Oelwein became a possibility, public school administrators chartered an airplane and visited model programs. School principals actively lobbied to have this program located in their community, and the local Superintendent of Schools, Elden Pile, took real professional risks to convince the local Board of Education to share in funding the project. Other innovative Oelwein programs have followed a similar pattern. It has been the Oelwein schools that have sparked interest in developing "therapeutic school suspension" and afterschool programs for at-risk youth. These programs later served as models for other Iowa communities. The result of this energy on the part of the public school administration has created a strong balanced partnership among Four Oaks, DHS, JCS, and the schools that in many ways has made Oelwein the strongest collaborative in Iowa's northern counties.

The accurate catchphrase here is, "Everyone must bring something to the table." This "something" can be dollars or staff time or expertise or effort. This "something" can be the simple willingness to share risk. But "investment" is more than a state of mind. It must include a willingness to commit important resources to the goals of the collaborative initiative.

"Orders From the Top"

In Iowa, as in other jurisdictions, nonhierarchical human services models will increasingly become our ideal, but bureaucratic and hierarchical organizational structures continue to define our reality.

For this reason, collaborative initiatives require strong mandates from top administrators to succeed. In addition, collaborative groups require highly visible modeling from top administrators to establish a parallel process as the context for collaboration.

In the early stage development of the PHASE Day Treatment Program, the district-level public and private administrators, Steve Smith, James Ernst, and Marlie Kasemeier established a clear top-down mandate: "This is a jointly owned project; collaboration is expected and required." More powerfully, these administrators modeled effective collaboration. If the top DHS, JCS, and private agency administrators could work together to create and fund this project, no less should be expected at a local level of collaborative management.

As Charles Bruner observes, "Collaboration at one level of organization will facilitate collaborating at other levels as well" [Bruner 1991]. Put negatively, "The killer barrier to cross-functional teams is a lack of managerial support" [Parker 1994].

Boundaries

To quote a well-known Robert Frost poem, "Good fences make good neighbors." As child welfare professionals, we know that the structure and safety provided by residential treatment is often necessary to allow troubled children to take new risks with relationships and to learn, grow, and change. Similarly, limits needs to be clarified and tested behaviorally within collaborative organizations if real trust is to grow.

Successful collaboration focuses on close relationships, new intimacy, and new integrations among collaborators, both as individuals and as organizations. Closeness, in turn, involves risk.

Interview respondents emphasized the ideals of closeness and "oneness" as they described their successful experiences in collaborative work. Kevin Wahl, a Waterloo JCS Supervisor, puts it this way: "It is ultimately a matter of trust. At some point, we all really own the project; it becomes ours, not theirs or mine."

However, interview responses also make it clear that authentic collaboration entails an equally realistic fear of being harmed by the process itself. As one JCS supervisor disclosed, "You know all of our secrets now, but I don't think I know all of yours." It is no accident that our human services organizations and systems have separated and disconnected. Threatening this equilibrium raises realistic fears of being exploited, victimized, personally and professionally embarrassed, or unwittingly "selling out" the legitimate needs and prerogatives of one's own organization.

As Bruner ironically points out, Webster's secondary definition of "collaboration" is "to cooperate with an enemy invader." Benedict Arnold is the case example. Collaboration is not a process where participants feel free from potential damage. The fact is that collaborative initiatives threaten the status quo. This essentially democratic structure challenges the hierarchy of each member's parent organization. It may also challenge the tenets of our professional identity as social workers, educators, or juvenile justice professionals. More practical and free-floating problem solving may threaten the psychological and bureaucratized "rule books" that make work safe—whether those rule books are real or imaginary [Bruner 1991].

What are the boundary conditions? This question needs to be successfully asked and answered in the context of each developing collaboration. There is great value in accomplishing explicit, boundary-setting work on the front end of every collaboration's formulation.

In the PHASE Day Treatment Program, administrative partners made a strong commitment from the beginning to foster empowered comanagement groups for each community program at a local level in Oelwein, Waterloo, and Dubuque. At the same time, a formal legal contract was put into place at the district level that specified such practical aspects of program definition as staffing ratios, payment rates, and credentials for staff. The contract also clarified a critical boundary for the public-private partnership. Public agency collaboration, even at the level of comanagement, could not entail a guarantee of referrals. Instead, the new program needed to stand on its own merits. In the real political context that existed at that time, this explicit rule protected both Four Oaks and public agencies from legitimate criticism from competitive private agencies, who felt that the PHASE collaboration could create unfair competitive advantages.

In theory, contractual and front-end boundary settings recommend themselves as effective tools for success. In reality, the need to establish clear boundaries will inevitably reoccur as the collaborative work evolves.

In the PHASE Day Treatment Program, early discussion in each local comanagement group emphasized mutual endorsement of a confrontational counseling approach with delinquent youth. When the reality of this practice created philosophical conflicts with parents and within the community, frank and explicit discussion was required to get beyond generalities and define both the acceptable limits of clinical practice and the boundaries of each collaborative's risk in a much more concrete way.

Clear Goals

Each collaborative must establish clear goals to achieve desired results. Sharon Kagan teaches us, "The final element essential to comprehensive service integration is the specification of targeted accomplishments. Service integration efforts must be guided by results-driven models that specify clear accomplishments" [Kagan et al. 1995]. In terms of our present discussion, goals function as an essential structuring element for the collaborative process.

Because of the nature of cross-system, interorganizational partnerships, members of the group may be in significant conflict with each other about a number of important issues. In the Iowa experience, organizational conflict is never far beneath the surface regarding, for example, the issue of "group care versus prevention." JCS staff would prefer to expand the use of structured residential placements because of this organization's adherence to a philosophy of behavioral accountability and an organization mission that emphasizes community safety. DHS, by contrast, leans in the direction of more cost-effective community-based services that focus on families, rather than individual children. Private agencies tend to polarize on this issue, based on whether they are primarily family-centered service providers, group care providers, or both.

These conflicts would be trivialized if considered as merely an issue of personalities or personal philosophy. Instead, they are powerful organizational dilemmas that relate to key cultural values and central organizational goals. Any meaningful collaborative program in Iowa's child welfare arena will tap the strong feelings and organizational conflicts that are attached to this issue.

Direct commitment to clearly stated goals becomes a powerful tool to minimize tension and to contract for cooperation in this context of potential conflict. It needed to be explicitly stated, for example, that the purpose of Waterloo's Logan Avenue Wrap-Around Project was not to resolve Iowa's group care funding issues. Instead, the purpose of the collaboration was to develop and manage a flexible, innovative, successful program.

In early planning, the PHASE Day Treatment Program was put forward as an alternative to institutionalization and group care. Group care dollars were, indeed, diverted to the PHASE program as an investment toward achieving this outcome. Considerable discussion was required among the partners to agree that Four Oaks, as the private agency that provided the day treatment service, could not subscribe to this goal statement. Utilization patterns for group care was a process and outcome beyond the scope of a single day treatment project or Four Oaks as a single agency. A more realistic goal was framed as "admitting and sustaining group care-level clients."

The real danger in the goal-setting process is that discussion will be superficial. Hard work is required to confront real differences and negotiate the pragmatic and altruistic goals that truly bring the collaborative together.

Concrete Tasks

William Glasser often asserted that talking about problems turns out to be an ineffective way to improve relationships. Delinquent boys and their fathers, he argued, benefit less from conventional therapy and more from spending time together fixing old cars. "Mutual, effortful action," Glasser maintains, creates connection [Glasser 1967].

In our work with many collaborative initiatives here in Iowa, we have found this therapy principle to be true. Collaborative groups that more or less approximate traditional "boards of governance" tend to fail or be relatively irrelevant in their impact. Collaborative groups that accomplish real hands-on work together tend to succeed.

In Waterloo's Logan Avenue Wrap-Around Project, public and private agencies meet together to review specific cases and develop innovative solutions to the challenges of maintaining a troubled youth in the community.

In the PHASE Day Treatment Program, community boards consider policy and review program operations, then reconvene to serve as the intake and utilization review team for the day treatment program.

At the Dubuque day treatment collaborative, which has embraced new projects, the function of the collaborative board has been extended to hiring key staff.

The point here is simple and powerful. Talking about things has a limited meaning in terms of trust and connection. Doing things together unites people and organizations.

Peer Networking

Like any human system, a collaborative group benefits from external inputs. In the Iowa experience, we have derived substantial value from structuring opportunities for collaborative groups to meet with others that are partnering on similar projects in other jurisdictions.

In the PHASE Day Treatment Program, representatives from Oelwein, Waterloo, and Dubuque have met on a quarterly basis to address common problems and to learn from one another's success, both in terms of program operations and collaborative work.

On a statewide level, Iowa Attorney General Tom Miller has established a Task Force on Juvenile Crime that serves not only as a state policy forum, but also as an opportunity for participants to share innovative, community-based prevention initiatives.

In developing the DHS/DECAT initiative, local DECAT coordinators network on a district and state level to review policy, to solve problems, and to learn from each other's experiences.

These opportunities for peer consultation open up the local collaborative to receive new information, obtain feedback, and borrow successful tools. Such opportunities also nurture informal peer support networks and reinforce the critical values underlying the movement toward more collaborative organizational designs.

Data and Outcomes

Focus on measurable results is, on the one hand, simply a matter of good management. In addition to grounding the work of the collaborative on an empirical basis, objective data and emphasis on outcomes serve as a powerful structural element to unify a diverse, and potentially divisive, membership around demonstrable results. Agreement on values, purpose, and vision all can have a similar structural effect, but these elements are conceptual and imprecise, and for this reason they may mask subtle misalignment and conflict. Data, by contrast, are concrete and, therefore, uniquely powerful.

In the PHASE Day Treatment Program, several important statistical indicators have been developed to quantify important program outcomes. Program retention rate quantifies whether or not these programs really sustain "residential-level youth" in a community-based setting. Program census quantifies both the fiscal health of the program and its credibility with direct service workers. Parent satisfaction surveys offer one means of objectifying the degree to which each program successfully implements its family-focused mission.

Once again, results-oriented and data-driven management is simply good management practice. The main point here is that developing and organizing the collaborative around objective data helps to unify a diverse membership and provide an objective basis, rather than a political and subjective basis, both for measuring success and for focusing collaborative effort.

Executive Control Function

Formal authority is an important structural issue for any organization. Family therapists, especially structural therapists, strongly emphasize the importance of executive control within the family system [Minuchin 1974]. Due to the essentially democratic and egalitarian thrust of collaborative work, the importance of the executive role assumes especially important—and often problematic—structural impact.

The executive function is not synonymous with power and control. The point is not "who is running the show." The fact is that, typically, most critical organizational, fiscal, and political components of power will be far beyond the control of any local collaborative. Instead, the point is that one person or agency needs to assume leadership in terms of managing the structure and organization that makes a collaborative function effectively as a social organization. Someone needs to chair meetings, to structure agendas, to monitor follow-through on tasks, to lead the group in focusing work on relevant issues and managing conflict, and to represent the collaborative to external groups or agencies.

Trouble will result when the executive function in this limited and important sense is unclear. Work will not proceed efficiently, and the collaborative will feel disorganized. Focus, decisionmaking, and follow-through will become fluid and disjointed.

We must restate and emphasize this point. The critical issue is not power and control; the critical issue is skill and resources. Executive leadership requires considerable skill and a considerable investment in time. The decision of who should lead the group should be made carefully, addressing the concerns with this decision that will inevitably occur within the group.

Increased Inclusion

The overall momentum of each collaborative venture should be toward expanding the range of membership in the partnership. In the early stages of project development, there may be a positive value in keeping group membership small to maximize cohesion and support effective task completion. But as each project matures, members must make aggressive efforts to expand the scope of participation. As Kagan insists, "A key element that is necessary in comprehensive service integration is the participation of a wide range of governmental and nongovernmental players. New participants need to be aggressively and creatively recruited at every level within the project" [Kagan et al. 1995].

Although the DECAT projects in Waterloo, Oelwein, and Dubuque find themselves at different levels of developmental maturity, all projects used the "Mapping a New Direction" Community Forum to achieve the objective of increased inclusion. Each community has become more comfortable in its ability to work in a collaborative design and, indeed, each community has realized the benefits of this design. Each community has also used the Forum to reach out to others to bring together more resources to address the challenges each community confronts today and in the future.

In the Dubuque Day Treatment initiative, the Juvenile Judge challenged the program, believing that youth stayed too long in care and reached a plateau where continued placement seemed difficult to justify. This problem was effectively resolved when the community board invited the Judge to the table (literally) to review specific cases and develop a mutual plan to improve program operations to achieve the results she expected. At the same time, collaborative comanagers helped the judge to accept a more realistic expectation for length of stay in the program.

In the Waterloo community, public sector direct service workers communicated that the Day Treatment Program did meet administrative and client needs, but that it also created meaningful day-to-day problems for line workers. In response, membership in the governing collateral has expanded to include line workers from all participating agencies.

As Anne Gruenewald, a Four Oaks Administrator, reminds us, "We need to challenge ourselves to continue to invite in client families, attorneys, law enforcement people, line staff, and neighborhood groups. The fact is, even across systemic boundaries, we are all human service managers. After a while, we all begin to sound alike."

Tools That Work: Leadership Elements

Effective leadership is critical to any human organization: a family, a therapy group, or a community. For effective cross-system collaborations, this principle is doubly true. Collaborative groups pull together divergent stakeholders and have a high potential for disorganization, disaffiliation, and outright conflict. Furthermore, by operating outside the context of any one institutional structure, stable external supports that underpin and guide the work of the members simply do not exist. Skilled leadership, therefore, is a critical ingredient both to get work done and to nurture the health of the collaborative itself.

Taking Care of Business

Discussions of leadership lend themselves to abstract and intangible ideals: vision, empowerment, integration. Leadership, we are frequently reminded, is much more than mere management. By contrast, interviewees asserted that we do well *not* to underestimate the importance of efficiently managing the detailed day-to-day business of any collaborative group.

Since collaboratives operate outside the functional frameworks of each parent organization, few practical administrative supports exist. Who takes notes at meetings? Who prepares written agendas? Who types this work? Who generates outcome data? Who schedules meeting rooms? Who coordinates rescheduling when needed? Who chairs discussions? Who makes the coffee?

Evan Klenk, Waterloo DHS Area Administrator, was involved in the "Mapping a New Direction" Community Forum. As a high-level administrator, Evan embraced this project in a public and highly symbolic way to communicate his strong personal commitment to develop a more collaborative and community-based paradigm for human services in Blackhawk County. Evan communicated his intensity about the "Mapping" project by holding planning meetings in his formal conference room. Evan also paid extremely detailed attention to what some participants considered minor elements of the project. What is the exact wording of the brochure? How will discussion leaders record their results? How will the name tags be made? In this particular project, Mr. Klenk's focus on detail not only ensured the project's success, but, more significantly, established a message of commitment and in this way empowered the collaborative's work.

In the Iowa experience, we have discovered that failure to attend to basic organizational details will quickly breed frustration. Yet, no mechanism exists to automatically assure this function. Effective and strategic management of such details communicates one image of the collaborative's significance and organizational integrity. Haphazard execution of this work communicates another. All of these responsibilities will adhere to the person and agency who assumes the role of functional leadership for the collaborative group.

Formal Management Tools

A more complex issue is the leadership necessary to provide the formal business management tools and processes that are required for success. As Eric Flamholtz has observed, organizations go through predictable stages of development, just as children work through developmental stages, and just as families evolve through a predictable family life cycle [Flamholtz 1990]. One important aspect of this developmental curve is a greater reliance upon formal business management tools and a greater positive valuation of professional business managers as each organization grows in size and complexity.

These issues assume considerable significance when many organizations at different stages of development come together to do collaborative work. How does each organization respond when recommendations are made to create detailed work plans; to conduct sophisticated performance appraisal for employees of a small, innovative treatment program; to prepare a formal mission statement for the collaborative; and then work the mission statement through every member organization?

This is one of many flashpoints where organizational cultures may predictably collide. For small, entrepreneurial organizations, public and private, this kind of work will be viewed negatively and is likely to be labeled as bureaucratic, overly structured, and too time consuming. For large public and private organizations, such mechanisms are viewed as the "very air we breathe." In this context, the leaders of the collaborative group need considerable sensitivity.

In the small, rural Oelwein community, there is a relatively low tolerance for bureaucracy. Key players in collaborative groups know each other intimately through their day-to-day work experience and do not have large staffs of specialists who need to be coordinated through formal management structures. This cultural style does not imply a lack of effectiveness or a lack of sophistication. In one Oelwein meeting, for example, a decision was made to develop an afterschool program for troubled adolescents. A flip chart was brought in. Managers produced pocket calculators and developed a project proposal—including a budget—within the hour. This is a community of "doers," where important results can be accomplished quickly.

By contrast, when the Waterloo community endorsed the "Mapping a New Direction" Community Forum, a formal management process needed to evolve. As previously pointed out, Evan Klenk, the Waterloo DHS Area Administrator, assumed a key leadership position and strongly asserted that even this seemingly simple needs assessment actively needed to be viewed in the context of complex community dynamics. Other major planning activities were in progress: the federal Office of Juvenile Justice and Delinquency Prevention "comprehensive strategy" and President Clinton's summit on volunteerism. Planning the

Forum, therefore, required sophisticated integration. Committees and subcommittees were necessary and formal work plans with timelines needed to be developed. While some participants chaffed under this level of structure, Evan was correct in his assessment. High levels of managerial sophistication and the explicit employment of formal management tools were required for the Forum to succeed and to ensure that this project achieved its potential benefit.

The level of managerial sophistication for each unique collaborative group needs to be geared to the complexity of the project. It is unwise to approach a complex program without a detailed work plan, especially when many organizations may need to integrate their work in intricate ways. On the other hand, it is silly to create a work plan that dwarfs the project.

Leadership awareness includes balancing the way divergent organizational cultures come together. The effective leader, like the Federal Reserve Bank, will lean against the wind of both large bureaucratic organizations that tend to overmanage and small entreprenuerial organizations that manage too little.

Vision

Leaders must communicate a cogent vision, both for the project and the process of collaboration itself. As Sue Davison, the Dubuque DECAT Coordinator, describes that program's process, "Tom and Gary have a clear picture of what this community, working together, should look like, and they talk this vision to every group and every organization, again and again and again."

Since the concept of "vision" has become almost a cliché in the world of business management and organizational development, it is worth emphasizing that "vision" has special significance in the world of collaborative work that involves the coming together of multiple disciplines, multiple agencies, and multiple organizational cultures, each bringing together different pictures of what each partnership arrangement is or needs to be.

What characterizes a strong vision statement? One well-recognized management text emphasizes four points [Belgard 1990]:

- **First, the vision statement should be clear.** Four Oaks managers often use one-page handouts that contain a simple diagram and invariably use the same handout with a wide range of stakeholder groups in order to, literally, put everyone "on the same page."

- **Second, the vision statement should be inspirational.** A good community-based treatment program, such as Waterloo's Logan Avenue Wrap-Around Project, may save money—but the better vision statement will emphasize the ethical value of keeping children united with their families.

- **Third, the vision statement needs to be credible and authentic.** It is hard to inspire consensus and integrated effort when leaders do not believe what they are saying.

- **Fourth, the vision statement should be realistically supported.** If there is no higher level managerial support in terms of resources or commitment for the vision on the part of constituent organizations, participants in the collaborative are set up to fail.

Good leaders will use the vision statement for the project throughout the life of the collaborative, not merely to clarify purpose at the onset. Especially as membership turns over, conflicts are confronted, or the collaborative loses focus, leaders need to hold up a picture of "how we have agreed we want things to be."

Impasses and Breakthroughs

In the Iowa experience, effective leaders have distinguished themselves by possessing a sensitive attention to timing. When the work of the collaborative is moving along nicely, good leaders know when to recede into the background and let empowerment occur. Good leaders also assert a stronger role at points of impasse, when the collaborative "gets stuck."

Steve Smith, the Chief Juvenile Court Officer for Iowa's 11 northern counties, demonstrates strong delegation skills in his administrative style. He has a reputation for responding to those seeking his administrative intervention by saying, "I leave that issue to Kevin (the local manager)." Less obvious is Smith's ability to keep a finger on the pulse of each local collaborative and to be physically and emotionally present when the going gets tough. This visible, direct, and consistent personal support has been critical to the success of many projects documented in this report.

Good leaders assert their centrality to celebrate breakthroughs and major victories in the collaborative effort. Once again, the insight here is understanding the unique challenge of collaborative work. Successful individual organizations develop strong reward systems: salary increases, promotions, bonuses, informal rewards. Collaboratives lack such built-in incentives. A good leader must make sure rewards are provided by praise within the group, by positive communications to parent organizations, and through recognition by key externals.

One strategic purpose in organizing the Community Forums in the "Mapping a New Direction" project has been to bring state and national leaders to Oelwein, Waterloo, and Dubuque to formally recognize success in collaboration to provide innovative programs. Early on in the PHASE Day Treatment Program, site visitations were orchestrated involving high-ranking state officials, such as Attorney General Tom Miller. As this report is written, the Dubuque Day Treatment collaborative has been chosen to make a presentation at a national Best Practices in Juvenile Justice Symposium in Kentucky.

Process Feedback

As previously noted, strong leaders develop a vision not only for the "product" of the collaborative, but also for the collaborative process itself. One important leadership function is to periodically help the collaborative group reflect upon its own process, offer each other feedback, and establish goals for how members and member organizations can relate more effectively.

For those of us with roots in the family therapy and residential team treatment environments, this kind of work has clear and obvious value. But it is important to realize that collaborative groups do not offer the level of safety or systemic integrity enjoyed by families or residential treatment teams. For this reason, resistance may be strong.

The PHASE Day Treatment Program in Iowa's northern counties allows delinquent youth to experience in a flexible manner four phases of treatment structure: residential care, two levels of day treatment, and intensive aftercare. In designing the program model, members reached a consensus that families, private agency program staff, and public agency case workers would "partner" to make decisions to move youth along this continuum.

As we discovered, "the devil was in the details." Process feedback revealed that each local jurisdiction was viewing this partnership quite differently. In Waterloo, JCS workers with high caseloads felt that Four Oaks program staff, who were seeking to include JCS staff in decision making, were inappropriately adding responsibility, time, and work—in fact, abdicating their own roles and responsibilities. In Oelwein, Four Oaks program staff who changed a youth's program status, even in an emergency situation, were viewed as too independent and failing to partner.

The issue here is not right or wrong. What is important to understand is that "click phrase" generalities can mask huge conflicts and that every partnership must be defined in a local context. Moreover, it is *only* an intentional priority to create process feedback discussion that will resolve such dilemmas.

One northern Iowa collaborative, the Logan School Project, has utilized a systematic team development process, emphasizing process feedback and using a structured model familiar to one member organization. Project staff regularly hold frank discussions of the collaborative's work in three areas: Is the project working smoothly? Is the project achieving stated outcomes? Are constituents' expectations being met? This discussion process has increased group cohesion and clearly contributed to the effectiveness of the work. More important, this level of self-awareness created culture change beyond the project. Prior to the Logan Project, many believed that agency turf was too strong for effective collaboration. As Denise Dunne, Waterloo DECAT Coordinator, relates, "The Logan Project changed this kind of negative expectation. It proved that local agencies know how to work together."

Breaking Barriers

A key leadership skill is the ability to address and resolve critical barriers that block a project's success or a collaborative group's course of development. Barrier breaking can be done in a dramatic and public way that champions the collaborative's value and consolidates the leader's position. This work can also be defined by a quiet facilitation that occurs behind the scene and that empowers the democratic process of the collaborative as a whole.

Lack of leadership in this important area is a too-common part of all of our experience. Projects falter because critical problems remain unresolved. The group becomes understandably discouraged as they continually confront and lament problems that seem beyond their control.

In Waterloo, the "Mapping a New Direction" planning group began to feel almost cursed by bad luck, in that national resource persons began to cancel their commitments to make presentations at the Forums for legitimate and unavoidable reasons. (One speaker, for example, fell and suffered a concussion just days prior to the conference.) In each situation, one leader aggressively approached the national or state agency to advocate for the local event and to ensure that some way was found to provide a credible replacement.

In planning the Forums in all three Iowa communities, an unfortunate pattern became clear. Local DECAT coordinators, by default, absorbed huge planning responsibilities for the detail work needed to carry off these events. In response to this problem, Jan Pratt, the "Mapping a New Direction" Comanager for this initiative, unobtrusively (but strategically) provided support by helping to develop timelines, sharing model agendas from one community to another, even helping to print name tags and fill conference folders in the last frantic minutes of preparation.

Defining leadership as "breaking barriers" is one potent method for empowerment. The leader does not invest energy in controlling the internal activities of the collaborative group. Instead, the leader directs his or her energy outward, addressing the problems that block the collaborative's success.

Challenge and Demand

Hirschhorn and Gilmore, in their study of cross-functional work teams, draw attention to the authority vacuum that can too often occur as organizations move toward increased collaboration and away from traditional, authoritarian, and controlling management styles. "When leaders abdicate authority, they cannot structure participation, teamwork, or empowerment effectively; this makes it impossible for teams to be productive" [Hischhorn & Gilmore 1992]. In some situations, this vacuum of authority is filled by too much group cohesion. Teams "get along," but work does not get done. At other times, team members may become paralyzed by conflicts and anxieties that, in the absence of strong leadership, cannot be safely expressed or productively resolved.

The Waterloo PHASE Day Treatment Program reached a critical impasse in program development. This treatment program was experiencing substantive performance problems. Poor hiring decisions had been made and high-risk situations had occurred among staff and clients. A chaotic environment that was disconcerting to client families, referring workers, and direct care staff developed. More significantly, the paralysis identified by Hirschhorn and Gilmore had begun to occur among the managerial staff collaborating to provide leadership for this project. High levels of conflict emerged and staff took sides to assign political blame for program failures. Working through this conflict, expressing ideas directly, and developing solutions had begun to seem unlikely to happen.

Steve Smith, JCS District Chief, and Jim Ernst, Four Oaks CEO, took the risk of an emphatic and authoritative leadership move. Program managers and the collaborative Board of Governors for the Program were essentially confronted with a high-level administrative vote of "no confidence." A treatment administrator external to the project was brought in to provide a comprehensive and formally documented program evaluation with specific recommendations for corrective action. This report was publicly and ceremoniously presented to the Program management team and to the governing board with a unified directive from public and private top administrators that corrective action must be promptly taken. As part of this intervention, two senior private agency managers were formally disciplined and removed from the project.

In the Oelwein Day Treatment Program, a similar need emerged for high levels of confrontation and demand from top-level agency administration. Conflicts had developed in the governing board regarding the proper boundaries for discipline and behavior treatment with delinquent youth. At a program level, direct care staff polarized around these issues in a highly toxic way, as they brokered what position they might take in response to the next predictable complaint.

Once again, Hirschhorn and Gilmore's metaphor of paralysis has real resonance in the Oelwein situation. No one felt safe. Hostilities were overtly expressed, but seldom resolved. No work was done toward consensual resolution of these problems. One key Four Oaks administrator executed strong leadership. He convened a meeting of the Board and confronted this collaborative with the probable consequences of continued failures to act: rapid staff turnover, increased community complaints, and the ultimate discrediting and failure of the program. Participants were challenged to specifically commit to do what they could to improve what was frankly labeled as a crisis situation. The Oelwein collaborative rose to the occasion. They made and kept commitments and resolved their problems.

As Hirschhorn and Gilmore accurately conclude, authority in the context of collaboration "is not about control, but it is about containment." The authoritative exercise of leadership is not directed toward making people do what the leader wants. It is directed toward the critical anxieties and hostilities that must inevitably arise in collaborative work. The purpose is to free participants to engage in real dialogue and to energize them to do real work.

Tools That Work: Interpersonal Elements

As the "Mapping a New Direction" interview respondents repeatedly emphasized, successful collaboration is ultimately an interpersonal phenomenon, a matter of specific people in a specific place and time learning to work together in a new way. Nonetheless, we would argue that effective collaboration requires more than good interpersonal skills and more than an individual commitment to cooperate. In collaborative work, partners come to the table not as independent individuals, but as representatives of their parent organizations. It is not enough for individuals to connect. If the collaborative is to succeed, organizations must integrate. For this reason, our challenge is to translate the well-recognized attributes of good personal relationships (trust, honesty, respect) into organizational terms and to explore what these words mean in the context of partnering agencies.

Personalities Matter

While success is clearly not simply a function of the mix of individual personalities that make up the collaborative, interview respondents emphasized again and again how individual personality traits must be viewed as one key piece of the collaboration puzzle:

"It was Tom's patience that really got us through the hard places." "It was Sue's optimism that helped the rest of us believe we could do it." "Art's flexibility has always been critical to our success." "It was Steve's support that made the difference." "None of this could have been accomplished without Jan's hard work, organization, and persistence." "Bill is the glue that holds it all together."

The fact is that some people partner better than others. We can identify some of the relevant skills: flexibility, openness, patience, interpersonal sensitivity, communication skills. Such skills can be learned and taught. However, existential qualities often become the real issue: courage, ability to take risks, the willingness to extend trust, the willingness to do things in a new way. Mike Mitchell, a Four Oaks Therapy Supervisor, makes this point: "I want my partners to be people who have the courage to change."

One or two strong individuals in key roles can spark a collaborative effort. Conversely, one or two of the wrong people can pose significant barriers to success. Therefore, choosing the organizational representatives who are selected to form a collaborative group becomes a set of decisions that should never be underestimated.

Like individuals, some organizations partner better than others, due to organizational capabilities, culture, and style. Agencies, like individuals, differ in terms of flexibility, responsiveness, and resources that can be shared. As with individuals, existential qualities also come into play: commitment, a willingness to take risks, the willingness to extend trust, and the willingness to do things in a new way.

Again, one or two strong organizations can carry a collaborative; inclusion of the wrong agencies can ensure failure.

Organizational Respect

Partnerships must be grounded in a climate of mutual respect. At a personal level, this is simply a matter of sound professional ethics and good common sense. Good partners never attack one another or say negative things behind each other's back. Partners treat one another with courtesy, decorum, and kindness. In an ideal world, this principle should go without saying. In the real world, it needs to be said, and said strongly. Sue Pitts-Fisher, a Four Oaks Supervisor, recounts an example that may be all too familiar. "It was disconcerting. I went to a meeting and the people were socializing before it started. Everyone was complaining in a really vicious way about Richard. Then Richard came in, so they started in on Jane. I learned one thing. Never be late for a meeting!"

On an organizational level, respect needs to be more closely defined as respect for diversity within the framework of collaboration.

When business leaders, educators, client families, and human services professionals come to the table to work together, cultures collide. As a result, there is a real tendency to label "different" as "wrong" and to respond to problems with blame and attack, rather than with a strong commitment to seek mutual understanding and common ground.

On a practical level, this is often no more than a matter of being "politically correct" in a sensitive way. For example, I will occasionally use profanity, strategically, to create emphasis. However, religious leaders played an important role in the Dubuque "Mapping a New Direction" planning group. Only after several uncomfortable silences did it become clear that these words were being interpreted as disrespectful to an important partner.

Respect demands that each member of the collaborative devote considerable time to understanding the norms and values of their partners' organizational culture. Teachers, for example, tend to value continued education, advanced degrees, and professionalism. Probation officers, in contrast, may value such personal characteristics as strength, "savvy," and experience. When educators use the word "paraprofessionals" in a condescending tone to describe teacher aides, JCS administrators will react negatively. And when probation officers casually describe traditionally trained professionals as easily manipulated by delinquent youth, we will not be surprised when the school principal in the collaborative group takes offense.

Organizational Nurture

Stephen Bavelak has defined nurture as "an empathic understanding of another person's basic needs and positive actions to ensure those needs are met." This understanding is powerful and captures the nurturing relationship between mother and child [Bavelak 1985].

This same kind of nurture needs to define the relationships between members of the cross-system collaborative. Once again, nurture needs to work organizationally as well as interpersonally. In our experience, good partners work hard to emphatically understand each other as people. They also work to understand each other's organizational "life-

and-death" issues. With this understanding, partners can relate to one another's basic needs and their attendant vulnerabilities with both sensitivity and respect.

In one collaborative program, private agency staff routinely provided late, poor-quality documentation. Agency staff responses to the problem were predictable: "This is just bureaucratic stuff—kids and programs are what is really important." This logic does make sense; children are more important than paper. However, this attitude and behavior (late documentation) communicates a huge failure to partner. As Pam Brown, an Oelwein DHS Supervisor relates, "Private agencies sometimes have no idea how damaging late documentation is to their relationships. DHS workers have to testify in court, and without documentation we end up looking like fools. More important, we know things a program may not know. More than once, late reporting has resulted in significant safety issues for kids and families."

At one point in the PHASE Day Treatment Program, a transfer of funds created extreme pressures on DHS residential treatment budgets in all three local jurisdictions: Oelwein, Waterloo, and Dubuque. DHS representatives asked that brief residential treatment be used sparingly as the behavior control "back-up" to community-based day treatment. This request caused Four Oaks program staff considerable anxiety—for good reason. Less behavioral control with delinquent youth would stress staff, children, and program. Empty beds in the residential program dedicated to this purpose would stress budget. On an organizational level, the nurturing response was to absorb this stress and take positive action to help partners meet key needs.

The PHASE Day Treatment Program unexpectedly caused the confrontational disciplinary practices that are common to residential treatment with delinquent youth to become more visible in community-based settings. As a result, these programs became politically controversial in a way that threatened Four Oaks as an agency. The easy solution (and the traditional solution for public agencies) would have been for the public agency partners to keep their distance. Instead, like a nurturing parent, Steve Smith, the District JCS Administrator, was highly visible in his support for confrontational, but professionally managed, forensic treatment philosophy.

Organizational Disclosure

Self-disclosure is a powerful dynamic in any relationship. Collaborative relationships are no exception. Direct, open communication develops trust and connection. Secrecy and "playing the cards close to the vest" creates distance and suspicion. As Sidney Jourard observes in *Disclosing Man to Himself*, "What is ultimately required here is the courage to risk vulnerability" [Jourard 1968].

As with any group, self-disclosure is not unimportant on a personal level. When participants share openly, group cohesion and effectiveness are more likely to follow. But once again, the important issue in cross-system collaboration is organizational. It is organizational self-disclosure that has primary significance.

In the Iowa experience, frank discussions of sensitive staff issues have provided important opportunities for organizational self-disclosure. Traditionally, in our roles as peer agencies, customers, or providers, disclosure of perceived problems with staff would be considered disloyal. We tend to support our staff "come hell or high water." In collaborative work, we have learned to share relevant staff issues with our partners and seek their help in supporting a poor worker's growth, discipline, or even termination. This appears to be an obvious thing to do in a comanagement structure. The reality is that it can be quite difficult and entails major risks.

Financial operations provide another critical venue for organizational self-disclosure. In the world of child welfare and juvenile justice, fiscal information is ultimately a matter of public record. At an experiential level, however, dollars are to organizations what sex lives are to individuals. These have traditionally been intimate issues seldom discussed in public. In our collaborative work in northern Iowa, however, public and private agencies have grown accustomed to putting their budgets on the table and freely sharing financial information and dilemmas. It is, in fact, not unusual for one agency manager to call a financial technician or CEO of another agency directly to request data to solve a problem. The result is an exponential increase in trust.

Organizational Trust

In the context of collaborative initiatives, our interview respondents suggest that trust is most effectively established through reliable follow-though on critical tasks. As Hirschhorn and Gilmore emphasize in their discussion of "boundaryless" corporations, the whole question of "who does what work" becomes a fluid issue when cross-functional teams replace traditional hierarchical structures. Task responsibility becomes less frequently predetermined by static roles and static functions. Instead, work must be carved up in increasingly creative and specialized ways. As a result, "Individuals must depend on others who have skills and resources they cannot control and often do not even understand, in order to get their own work done" [Hirschhorn & Gilmore 1992]. In this kind of highly interdependent work environment, trust in one another's ability to consistently follow though on tasks becomes a critical issue.

Kevin Wahl, the Waterloo JCS Supervisor, makes this point in a succinct way. "The proof," he observes, "is in the pudding." Folks may get along together nicely and participate effectively in meetings, but the people who earn trust are those who routinely deliver the critical results.

On the organizational level, individuals come to the table as representatives of organizations, so generally it is organizations that accomplish the tasks that are significant for collaborative work—not one individual. Therefore, the focus of our thinking about trust is less about the relationships between members, and move importantly on the relationships between each member of a collaborative and her or his parent organization.

An organizational representative may highly value a collaborative project and commit to tasks that will ensure the project's success. If, however, the parent organization fails to support that commitment, the project may fail. This situation erodes trust and devalues the collaborating individual. In other situations, an organizational representative may simply be insufficiently empowered by the parent organization to effectively partner in a collaborative group. Every decision must be taken back for internal review and decision making. Whether such reviews are routinely favorable or not, the disempowered representative is unlikely to become a trusted member of the group.

From an organizational perspective, establishing trust becomes a matter of resources and of risk. Not only must an organization be willing to invest important resources in the collaborative's work, it must also invest time to assure that the organizational representative possesses the information and the latitude to act as an empowered custodian of the resources in question. In addition, the parent organization establishes trust by taking the risk that their representative, in the collaborative process, will commit these resources wisely.

As Gary Lippe, Dubuque County DHS Director, points out, "One major issue for me is whether or not I can trust my partners to honor their commitments and follow though, especially when the going gets tough within their own organization. Will they fight the necessary internal battles? Do they really have the ability to keep their commitments? Do they have the support of their internal hierarchy, or are they fighting their own internal command structure every step of the way?"

Strength-Based Approach

In collaboration work, members do not naturally come to the table with a positive attitude toward their partners. Child welfare systems, schools, public agencies, private agencies, welfare department, and juvenile probation have a long tradition of blaming each other for their own problems and for children's problems as well. As Bruner states, the first act of faith that is often required in any collaborative is the willingness to stop the practice of "viewing other agencies as part of the problem" [Bruner 1991].

Moving our orientation from blame to respect to a strength-based approach is a difficult process—one that is too often trivialized and discounted by experienced, pragmatic managers. What is required is not merely being nice or "cheerleading," but rather the courage to honestly analyze our own work without projection of blame and to connect with our partners in a way that mobilizes their strengths in terms of the work at hand. This calls for both interpersonal sensitivity and self-awareness. Individuals who genuinely internalize this orientation are a great gift to any collaborative group.

In our experience, it is unlikely that an organization will take a strength-based orientation toward its collaborative partners when that organization's overall culture is negative and distrustful of clients and their own staff. Organizations that consciously strive toward a strength-based orientation in all aspects of their work will most effectively and credibly bring this quality to their collaborative relationships as well.

In initiating delinquency-specific day treatment programs in northern Iowa, our treatment philosophy has incorporated a strength-based definition of partnering with client families. This has not been a soft-minded or naive approach. Instead, this practice principle demonstrates a full and sophisticated understanding that parents of delinquent children may present severe problems and have antisocial orientations themselves. Nonetheless, program staff are helped to not blame and attack parents or try to compete with them. Further, the program itself does not "treat" parents in the belief that this treatment would alter the irresponsible behaviors of older delinquent adolescents. Instead, program staff seek to partner with parents as adult peers who love their children, want what is best for them, and have considerable positive strengths to bring to bare on the shared task of helping their troubled child make real changes.

The value of this family-based treatment philosophy can certainly be debated. But this program's strength-based philosophy has helped set the tone for collaborative relationships among the agencies that collaboratively provide this program. If this tough-minded, yet strength-based approach is the model for how program staff should partner with families, why should partnerships among agencies be fundamentally different?

While the main purpose of each of the "Mapping a New Direction" Community Forums was to widen the range of involvement in community planning, a secondary purpose was to specifically praise important community programs for their successful collaborative work. Planners helped high-profile external authorities (including the Iowa Attorney General and representatives of CWLA) to praise real successes in a specific and credible way.

This process of celebrating excellence had its own independent value: when collaborative agencies work together for several months to achieve a result that embodies a strength-based perspective, that work cements those values and enables these same organizations to relate to each other in more positive ways.

Extending the Organization

Good partners respect appropriate boundaries, but they also extend themselves to show an interest in each other's work and volunteer to do work that does not have to be "theirs."

As Bruner has written, collaboration means more than communication and coordination of tasks. Collaboration implies a more flexible investment in achieving a common goal together [Bruner 1991]. Similarly, Hirschhorn and Gilmore point out that effective partnering entails not only a positive trust that the other members will do their part, but "taking a lively interest in the challenges and problems facing others who contribute in a different way to the final product or service" [Hirschhorn & Gilmore 1992].

On an interpersonal level, the required skill is the ability to walk the fine line between investment and overcontrol, between concern and intrusion. More importantly, the skill that is most required and most difficult to achieve is the ability to make the extra effort to assure a high-quality result without resentment or grandiosity. These are difficult emotional tasks to accomplish. As Bruner says, a frequent resistance to collaborative work is to say, "What! So now I have to do my job and their job too!" [Bruner 1991].

No better example of an individual who extends herself to assist collaborative partners could be found that Jan Pratt, District Decategorization Manager and a leader in the "Mapping a New Direction" initiative. With many pressing responsibilities on a district-wide level, Jan could have appropriately defined her role in providing Community Forums as detached and organizational in nature. Instead, her greatest contribution was to keep her finger closely on the pulse of those who carried out key tasks and, whenever necessary, to move in and help with any task that may be required: negotiating a developing conflict, facilitating a discussion group, stuffing envelopes, or tabulating information developed in each Forum. As important as Jan's work itself has been, the style with which her work has been done is even more instructive: never discounting, overcontrolling, or asserting ego, but always simply helping to get done what needed to get done.

The organizational characteristics required to promote this kind of individual investment are flexibility and an emphasis on results. When organizations, by policy and culture, prevent their staff from stepping outside their traditional functions and institutionally sanctioned expertise, collaborative work will be limited to coordination of traditional roles and work. When organizations value results and reward their staff for doing whatever is required to achieve success, real collaboration is more likely to occur. This emphasis on flexibility and results drives individuals to extend themselves beyond traditional role definition to support each other in achieving collaborative goals.

While the response of Iowa's law enforcement community has generally been positive in relation to recent community-based treatment initiatives for delinquent youth, it is also fair to say that local police departments are typically careful to protect their own resources and organizational boundaries. As one police captain in a large community asserted during a discussion of the need for police help in transporting out-of-control youth to secure settings: "We can't handle client control problems for you; our job is to prevent real crime." By contrast, from the beginning of the Oelwein Day Treatment Project, the Oelwein Police Department has defined their partnership by doing whatever is necessary (in a flexible way) for the project to succeed.

Early on in the project planning, Chief John Starky's support in meeting with such influential groups as the Chamber of Commerce and City Council was instrumental in alleviating community anxieties about programming for delinquent youth in an open community setting. In the first weeks of establishing the Day Treatment Project, Starky's visible presence, usually in full dress uniform, communicated a strong message of community support to both program staff and potentially limit-testing adolescents. As this rural day treatment initiative developed, a crucial pressure point evolved. The cost of transporting youth from nearby small communities prevented investment in tracking and monitoring programs for youth during the hours they were not supervised by program staff. The solution? Local police officers became far more effective than urban, agency-funded, tracker units in monitoring the activities of day treatment clients and reporting to program staff.

Organizational Investment

In *The Road Less Traveled*, Peck provides a wonderful definition of love. We wrestle with understanding what love means, Peck says, but we would do well by observing a boy with his first automobile. He drives it, washes it, polishes it, and tunes the engine. When he is not with this car, he thinks about it. And the car gets attended to. A tire that is only a few pounds low on pressure gets filled. The oil is changed more often than necessary. A dent or paint chip is quickly repaired. As Peck observes, "What a wonderful world it would be, if only we related to our children in just this way" [Peck 1978].

Partners in collaboratives need to take this same lesson. Successful collaboration entails the investment of time and attention to detail. As Sue Davison, the Dubuque DECAT Coordinator, related in her "Mapping a New Direction" interview, "It really may be no more than a matter of time, time, and more time—spending it together. The two key leaders of the Dubuque DECAT project go to meeting after meeting after meeting, even when they have more important things to do, even when the meetings don't relate to their agendas. The point is that their involvement is important to the other participants."

The negative side of this equation is common to all of us and easy to illustrate. We are all busy people, and the allocation of our time signals allocation of value. As a result, absence also sends a strong message. When people can't find time to come to meetings, the collaborative is in jeopardy.

As Bruner has pointed out, "Collaboration is time consuming. Communication needs to occur and the position, roles, and responsibilities of others need to be learned. This time must be added in when calculating caseload size or other responsibilities. Committed persons sitting through meetings discussing coordination or collaboration often privately ask themselves, 'Wouldn't it be easier for me to just do this myself?'" [Bruner 1991].

On an organizational level, the principle for practice is clear—and it is a hard message. Organizations must find time for staff to involve themselves in time-consuming collaborative activities. It is not enough to give lip service to valuing collaboration or to expect organizational leaders to learn to work in a new way. Time and responsibilities must be allocated specifically to support collaborative goals, and this, in turn, requires a financial investment.

The rural setting of Oelwein dramatizes an example of what too often can happen. In this small community of 6,000 people, the juvenile court representative to collaborative groups, Steve Buschbaum, is also a direct service probation officer with a full caseload—not a supervisor who attends meetings as a large part of his job. As Roger Downs, the JCS District Supervisor relates, "My staff are starting to hear 'collaboration' as a dirty word. I can't reduce their caseloads, but they feel required to attend an ever-increasing number of meetings." As a result of these state-driven organizational barriers, Mr. Buschbaum is forced to make a huge personal commitment to participate effectively in important collaborative work in the Oelwein community.

Four Oaks provides a positive instance of an organizational design intentionally crafted to allow time for collaborative work. Senior administrators and high-level service supervisors are assigned to and often located in designated geographic areas. One-third of their time is allocated to community work. However, while this design has provided great benefits, it may not be sustainable. As revenues are reduced and internal stresses increase, a major organizational challenge will be discovering ways for this high-level investment in community collaboration to realistically continue.

Conclusions

Iowa, like other states, is moving toward a new vision of how to provide help to troubled youth and troubled families—a vision that views children in the context of their families, emphasizes a community base and a neighborhood focus—a vision that provides a collaborative model for working together.

One intended message of this monograph is that Iowa has no magic answers, except that we think there is some value in understanding where we have been, where we are going, and what we have learned along the way.

Having said all this, if we were to give four pieces of specific advice to those taking on the difficult challenge of authentic collaboration, we would emphasize the following points:

- **Assess the state context.** The very nature of collaborative work can condemn us to tunnel vision. And when we focus too closely on interpersonal partnerships and center on the community, we may ignore the important dynamics of larger systems—at our own risk.

- **Think structure.** A collaborative initiative is not merely a collection of organizations getting together. The collaborative becomes its own group. All the wisdom we acquired about families, our own parent organizations, and our own communities must be applied to the collaborative as a unique entity with its own unique tensions, cohesion, rules, roles, subgroups, structure, and dynamics.

- **Emphasize leadership.** Collaboration implies equalitarian democracy. This makes leadership a hard issue. Nevertheless, skilled leadership is crucial is a collaborative is to succeed. How each collaborative resolves this dilemma will become one key to its success.

- **Nurture partners and their organizations.** One anonymous worksheet from a seminar on collaboration points out that "we must learn to recognize that we hold our partner's professional self-esteem in our hands." This is a good place to end our discussion. In spite of the real benefit of abstract analysis and business management theory, collaboration is, ultimately, simple a matter of people talking to people—a matter of trust. At one level, trust relates to reliability and follow-through. At a more fundamental level, empathic understanding of our partners' individual and organizational needs makes all the difference.

References

Bavelak, S., & Comstock, C. (1985). *A nurturing program for parents and children* (Parent handbook). Park City, UT: Family Development Resources, Inc.

Braziel, D. (1996). *Family-focused practice in out-of-home care.* Washington, DC: Child Welfare League.

Bruner, C. (1996). *Realizing a vision for children, families, and neighborhoods: An alternative to other modest proposals.* Des Moines, IA: National Center for Service Integration.

Bruner, C. (1991). *Thinking collaboratively: Ten questions and answers to help policy makers improve children's services.* Washington, DC: Education and Human Services Consortium.

Coleman, J. (1972). *Abnormal psychology and modern life.* New York: Scott, Foresman, and Company.

Flamholtz, E. G. (1990). *Growing pains: How to make the transition from a entrepreneurship to a professionally managed firm.* San Francisco, CA: Jossey-Bass.

Frost, R. (1936). *Complete poems of Robert Frost.* New York: Holt, Rinehart and Winston.

Funero, P., Nelson, R., & Pollack, J. (1998). *Briefings of the Iowa Human Services Restructuring Task Force.* Des Moines, IA: Legislative Service Bureau.

Glasser, W. (1967). *Schools without failures.* New York: Harper and Row.

Gruenewald, A. (1998). *Forging collaborative partnerships: The Waterloo Neighborhood Project.* Washington, DC: CWLA Press.

Hagebak, B. R. (1979). Local human services delivery: The integration imperative. *Public Management Forum, 39* (6), 575-582.

Hirschhorn & Gilmore. (1992, May). The new boundaries of the "boundaryless" company. *Harvard Business Review.*

Jouard, S. M. (1968). *Disclosing man to himself.* New York: Van Nostrand Reinhold Company.

Kagan, S. (1993). *Integrating services for children and families: Understanding the past to shape the future.* New Haven, CT: Yale University Press.

Kagan, S., Golub, S. A., Goffin, S. G., & Pritchard, E. (1995). *Toward systemic reform: Service integration for young children and their families.* Falls Church, VA: National Center for Service Integration.

Kalemkiarian, S. (1996). Forging alliances and breaking the boundaries: Serving "SED" kids in the juvenile justice system. Presentation made at the Mid-Year Technology Meeting 1996: "Juvenile Justice Challenges and Responsibilities." National Association of Psychiatric Treatment Centers for Children, Washington, DC.

Minuchin, S. (1974). *Families and family therapy.* Cambridge, MA: Harvard University Press.

Oss, M. E., & Taylor, C. (1997, October). A community reinvestment model for managed care: A look at two years of the Iowa program. *The Children's Vanguard,* 5-7.

Parker, G. M. (1994). *Cross-functional collaboration.* New York: Training and Development.

Peck, M. S. (1978). *The road less traveled.* New York: Simon and Schuster.

About the
Author

 James L. Hoel, B.A., has administered residential treatment, day treatment, and treatment foster care programs in Iowa for more than 25 years. He is Vice President for Juvenile Justice and Child Welfare Services at Four Oaks of Iowa, Inc., a private, nonprofit human service agency headquartered in Cedar Rapids, Iowa.

Family-Focused Practice in Out-of-Home Care: A Handbook and Resource Directory
Dennis J. Braziel, Editor

More and more, agencies that work with children and families are moving to develop an array of services that recognize the importance of maintaining and supporting the parent-child connection. *Family-Focused Practice in Out-of-Home Care* provides practical "hands-on" support to help agencies bring a family focus to their policy and administrative and program structures. The book goes further to describe the agency change process from a traditional out-of-home care agency to one that develops and improves relationships with families of children in care.

To Order: 1995/0-87868-635-5   Stock #6355 $18.95

Write: CWLA c/o PMDS   Call: 800/407-6273
        P.O. Box 2019   301/617-7825
        Annapolis Junction, MD 20701
e-mail: cwla@pmds.com   Fax: 301/206-9789

Please specify stock #6355. Bulk discount policy (not for resale): 10-49 copies 10%, 50-99 copies 20%, 100 or more copies 40%. Canadian and foreign orders must be prepaid in U.S. funds. MasterCard/Visa accepted.

CHILD WELFARE LEAGUE OF AMERICA

Forging Collaborative Partnerships: The Waterloo Neighborhood Project
Anne Gruenewald

Forging Collaborative Partnerships is designed to assist voluntary

agencies to develop the tools and strategies they need to move

toward a family-focused, community-based model for service

delivery to children in out-of-home care. It examines the experiences

that the community gained and outlines the methods that were used

to create an effective network of private/public partnerships.

To Order: 1998/0-87868-732-7   Stock #7327 $9.95

Write: CWLA c/o PMDS   Call: 800/407-6273
        P.O. Box 2019   301/617-7825
        Annapolis Junction, MD 20701
e-mail: cwla@pmds.com   Fax: 301/206-9789

Please specify stock #7327. Bulk discount policy (not for resale): 10-49 copies 10%,
50-99 copies 20%, 100 or more copies 40%. Canadian and foreign orders must be
prepaid in U.S. funds. MasterCard/Visa accepted.